DK WORKBOOKS

2nd Grade

Problem Solving

Author Linda Ruggieri

Educational Consultant Daniel Ottalini

DK

Penguin Random House

Senior Editor Cécile Landau
Editor Nishtha Kapil
US Editors Christy Lusiak, Allison Singer
Project Art Editor Dheeraj Arora
Senior Art Editor Ann Cannings
Art Director Martin Wilson
Producer, Pre-Production Nadine King
Producer Priscilla Reby
DTP Designer Dheeraj Singh
Managing Editor Soma B. Chowdhury
Managing Art Editor Ahlawat Gunjan

First American Edition, 2016
Published in the United States by DK Publishing
345 Hudson Street, New York, New York 10014

Copyright © 2016 Dorling Kindersley Limited
DK, a Division of Penguin Random House LLC
16 17 18 10 9 8 7 6 5 4 3 2 1
001–285371–Feb/2016

A catalog record for this book
is available from the Library of Congress.
ISBN: 978-1-4654-4452-3

DK books are available at special discounts when purchased
in bulk for sales promotions, premiums, fund-raising, or
educational use. For details, contact: DK Publishing Special
Markets, 345 Hudson Street, New York, New York 10014
SpecialSales@dk.com

Printed and bound in China.

All images © Dorling Kindersley Limited
For further information see: www.dkimages.com

A WORLD OF IDEAS:
SEE ALL THERE IS TO KNOW

www.dk.com

Contents

This chart lists all the topics in the book. Once you have completed each page, stick a star in the correct box below.

Learn to use a number line to add and subtract.

Use the number line to add or subtract. Write the number sentence you use and then the answer. The first one has been done for you.

Stacy planted 13 tomato plants. Barry planted seven lettuce plants. How many plants did they plant in all?

```
10   11   12   13   14   15   16   17   18   19   20
```

13 + 7 = 20   20 plants

On Monday, it snowed 6 inches in the town of Millbrook. On Tuesday, it snowed 7 inches. How much snow fell in those two days?

```
0   1   2   3   4   5   6   7   8   9   10   11   12   13
```

7 + 6 = 13   13 inches

There were 36 birds in a tree. After a while, three birds flew away. How many birds were left in the tree?

```
30   31   32   33   34   35   36   37   38   39   40
```

36 − 3 = 33   33 birds

Nicole collected 15 coins and Gary collected nine. How many more coins than Gary has Nicole collected?

```
5   6   7   8   9   10   11   12   13   14   15
```

15 − 9 = 6   6 coins

Learn to recognize numbers when they are written as words.

Find the number words from the box in the word search.

one		three		four		two		six
	hundred			seventeen			forty-five	
fifty		ninety		twelve		seventy		thirty

O	T	X	H	U	N	D	R	E	D	S	A	N
T	A	F	A	P	B	X	N	I	N	E	T	Y
H	F	O	R	T	Y	F	I	V	E	V	H	F
I	Y	W	P	O	T	W	E	L	V	E	R	O
R	T	S	E	V	E	N	T	E	E	N	E	U
T	W	I	O	N	E	I	D	U	X	T	E	R
Y	O	X	V	E	N	F	I	F	T	Y	R	A

Solve these addition problems. First write the answers in words and then in numbers.

thirty + twenty = ...   ⬭   eight + nine = ...   ⬭

ten + twenty = ...   ⬭   two + two = ...   ⬭

★ Number Words

Practice recognizing numbers when they are written as words.

Draw a line to match the number on the left to the correct number word on the right.

98	Three hundred three
400	Nine hundred six
125	Four hundred
906	One hundred twenty-five
303	Ninety-eight

Solve each problem. Write the answer first in number form and then in words.

Aunt Ruth cleaned her closet over the weekend. She gave away ten white sweaters and three black ones. How many sweaters did she give away in all?

◌ sweaters ....

David and Donald donated 36 nonfiction books and 25 fiction books to charity. How many books did they donate in all?

◌ books ....

Gabe is going through his toy car collection. He has decided to give away 20 blue cars and five red cars to his younger cousin. How many cars will Gabe give away altogether?

◌ cars ....

Learn the terms "addends" and "sums" used in addition.
Addends are numbers added together to equal a sum.

Write the addend that's missing from each number sentence.

1 + ⬚ = 10   ⬚ + 1 = 10   5 + ⬚ = 10

3 + ⬚ = 10   ⬚ + 3 = 10   6 + ⬚ = 10

2 + ⬚ = 10   ⬚ + 6 = 10   ⬚ + 2 = 10

Find the sum for each problem.

15 + 2 = ⬚   2 + 12 = ⬚   13 + 7 = ⬚

8 + 3 = ⬚   7 + 5 = ⬚   11 + 9 = ⬚

Read the story below and circle all the numbers of fruits mentioned in it.

Mark and Fiona went to the supermarket. They wanted to buy different kinds of fruit. They bought 4 apples and 6 bananas and put them in a bag. Next Mark and Fiona looked for other fruit. They bought 6 pears, 4 oranges, and 2 plums. Then they went home to make fresh fruit salad!

Now write the numbers you circled in the boxes below.
Finally, add them to find the sum, or the total number of fruits.

⬚ apples + ⬚ bananas + ⬚ pears + ⬚ oranges + ⬚ plums

= ⬚ fruits

★ Math Terms

Learn the words often used in math problems.

Use words from the word box to complete the crossword puzzle below.

ten	plus	number line	equal	minus	digit	total

Across

1. A line sometimes used to add or subtract

2. The number 12 is a two- .... number

7. Word for the symbol **+**

Down

3. Word for the symbol **–**

4. Another word for **sum**

5. Word for 10

6. Word for the symbol **=**

$\$\times\div\%=\$+?-\times\div\%=\$?+-\%\times\div=\$+?-\times\div\%$

Learn to solve problems that involve adding up to 20.

Solve these problems. First write the number sentence you use, then write the answer. The first one has been done for you.

Jack has a collection of rocks. He has 14 black rocks and four gray rocks. How many rocks does Jack have altogether?

14 + 4 = 18   18 rocks

Lola baked cupcakes for her classmates. She baked eight chocolate cupcakes and six vanilla ones. How many cupcakes did Lola bake altogether?

_____   ____ cupcakes

Pam has five history books and 12 science books on her bookshelf. How many books for both subjects does Pam have?

_____   ____ books

Tim and Andre are playing with their toy cars. Tim has eight cars, and Andre has 11 cars. How many toy cars do they have in all?

_____   ____ cars

GOAL

Learn to solve problems that involve subtracting two-digit numbers.

Figure out each answer. Write the number sentence you use and then the answer. The first one has been done for you.

A school garden has 15 plants. Mason watered 10 of them. How many more plants does he still have to water?

$$15 - 10 = 5$$ 5   plants

Hillcrest School has a new playground. It has 13 swings and 11 slides. How many more swings than slides are in the playground?

(....................)   (...)   swings

Mr. Isaac gave a puzzle book to every student in his class. He had 20 puzzle books. His class had 18 students. How many books were left over?

(....................)   (...)   books

Ms. Gordon has 20 students in her class. She sent ten students to the library. The rest worked at their desks. How many worked at their desks?

(....................)   (...)   students

Grace brought 24 cupcakes to school. She shared 18 cupcakes with her friends. How many cupcakes were left?

(....................)   (...)   cupcakes

Learn to spot key words in problems that can help you solve them.

Look at the words and phrases in the chart. Each one is a clue to let you know whether you need to add or subtract.

Add (+)	plus	altogether	in all	sum	total
Subtract (–)	minus	were left	more or fewer than	take away	difference between

Read the problems. Underline the key words and phrases that tell you to add or subtract. Then write number sentences to solve the problems and the answers. The first one has been done for you.

Clara's dog Muffin had a litter of puppies. She had three black puppies and four brown ones. How many puppies did Muffin have altogether?

> 3 + 4 = 7   7   puppies

Ron counted 28 children at the park. Kelly counted 15 adults there. How many more children than adults were at the park?

> [   ]   [   ] children

Jenny collected 21 white buttons, 35 silver buttons, and 10 gold buttons. How many buttons did she collect in all?

> [   ]   [   ] buttons

Atul brought 24 apple muffins to school. His friends ate 18 of them. How many muffins were left?

> [   ]   [   ] muffins

Hundreds, Tens, and Ones

Learn about the place values of hundreds, tens, and ones in three-digit numbers. For example, the number 234 is made up of 2 hundreds, 3 tens, and 4 ones.

Hundreds	Tens	Ones
2	3	4

For each number, write how many hundreds, tens, and ones it has in the box below.

789

Hundreds	Tens	Ones

100

Hundreds	Tens	Ones

906

Hundreds	Tens	Ones

453

Hundreds	Tens	Ones

634

Hundreds	Tens	Ones

230

Hundreds	Tens	Ones

Choose the correct number from above to solve each riddle below.

I am the number two hundred thirty.

I have no tens and no ones.

I am the number closest to 1,000.

I am a number greater than 453 but less than 789.

I can be added to 400 and the sum will be 853.

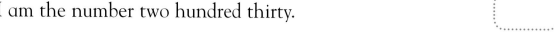

Hundreds, Tens, and Ones

Reinforce understanding of hundreds, tens, and ones (place value).

Circle the place value of the underlined digit.

6<u>1</u>	6 hundreds	6 tens	6 ones
29<u>7</u>	7 hundreds	7 tens	7 ones
<u>3</u>00	3 hundreds	3 tens	3 ones
4<u>5</u>3	5 hundreds	5 tens	5 ones
90<u>7</u>	7 hundreds	7 tens	7 ones

Read each problem and figure out the answer.

Subtract 2 ones from the number 356.

Add 5 tens and 3 ones to the number 723.

Add 2 hundreds to the number 296.

Subtract 2 tens and 6 ones from 829.

Add 3 hundreds, 2 tens, and 5 ones to the number 174.

GOAL

Learn to identify even and odd numbers. Even numbers end in 0, 2, 4, 6, or 8. Odd numbers end in 1, 3, 5, 7, or 9.

Count the objects in each row. Circle pairs of the objects.
Are the number of objects even or odd? Circle the answer.

even   odd

even   odd

even   odd

Read the sentences below. Underline the number or number word in each sentence. Is it even or odd? Circle the correct answer.

Jake's dad made three cups of hot chocolate.	even	odd
He filled a bowl with 12 marshmallows.	even	odd
Jenny put two marshmallows in her cup.	even	odd
Jake put five marshmallows in his.	even	odd
He popped one in his mouth. Yum!	even	odd

$x ÷ % = $ + ? − x ÷ % = $? + − % x ÷ = $ + ? − x ÷ %

Practice identifying even and odd numbers.

Jim is going fishing. Help him catch the nine fish with odd numbers on them by coloring them in.

Look at the numbers in the box. Write the even numbers on the bucket labeled **Even**. Write the odd numbers on the bucket labeled **Odd**.

7	2	3	4	5	20	34	6	106	57	8	9
210	23	68	11	12	13	14	46	15	155	97	31

Even   **Odd**

★ Regroup and Add

Learn to add two-digit numbers by regrouping. For example, 28 and 35 can be added as follows:

Add the ones → Regroup 13 ones into 1 ten and 3 ones → Add the tens 1 ten + 2 tens + 3 tens

```
   2 8              1              1
 + 3 5            2 8            2 8
 _____         + 3 5          + 3 5
    13          _____         _____
                   3             6 3
```

Regroup to solve the following addition problems.

```
   3 5          2 9          2 6          8 8
 + 4 7        + 1 1        + 3 4        + 1 2
 _____       _____       _____       _____


   3 5          5 8          1 4          4 5
 + 5 5        + 2 5        + 1 7        + 4 7
 _____       _____       _____       _____


   2 6          4 8          7 2          2 9
 + 4 7        + 3 8        + 2 9        + 3 8
 _____       _____       _____       _____


   9 2          2 5          1 8          1 9
 + 2 9        + 4 7        + 2 2        + 1 6
 _____       _____       _____       _____
```

$x\div\%=\$+?-x\div\%=\$?+-\%x\div=\$+?-x\div\%$

Learn to solve problems by regrouping and adding.

Cara, Jeff, and their mom were waiting at the airport to board their plane. Solve these problems. Show your work in the box. The first one has been done for you.

Cara counted 16 people waiting in a line. Jeff counted 25 people sitting in chairs. How many people did they count in all?

people

$$\begin{array}{r} 1 \\ 16 \\ + 25 \\ \hline 41 \end{array}$$

Jeff counted the number of children waiting at the airport. He counted 24 boys and 28 girls. How many children did he count in all?

children

Cara counted 18 books and 28 magazines on a book stand. How many books and magazines did she count in all?

books and magazines

Jeff bought 16 fruit bars at the snack stand. Cara bought three bottles of water and three bags of pretzels. How many items did they buy altogether?

items

Mom said they had waited 15 minutes. They had 35 minutes more before they could get on the plane. How long did they have to wait in total?

minutes

★ Regroup and Subtract

GOAL

Learn to subtract from two-digit numbers by regrouping.

Borrow 1 ten from the tens to make 15 ones → Subtract 6 ones from 15 → Subtract 2 tens from 3 tens

$$\begin{array}{r} \overset{3}{\cancel{4}}\overset{1}{5} \\ -\ 2\ 6 \\ \hline \end{array}$$
→
$$\begin{array}{r} \overset{3}{\cancel{4}}\overset{1}{5} \\ -\ 2\ 6 \\ \hline 9 \end{array}$$
→
$$\begin{array}{r} \overset{3}{\cancel{4}}\overset{1}{5} \\ -\ 2\ 6 \\ \hline 1\ 9 \end{array}$$

Solve these problems. Show your work in the box.
The first one has been done for you.

Dave and Gabby went to the beach to build a sand castle. Dave started the castle and built it seven inches high. Gabby then increased the height to 14 inches. How much taller did Gabby make the castle?

 inches

Gabby built eight steps going up the castle. Then Dave added more.
The total number of steps was 17.
How many steps did Dave build?

steps

Dave and Gabby made 26 little windows.
Of those, Gabby made eight. How many windows did Dave make?

windows

Dave filled his pail with 37 pebbles to place around the castle. Gabby filled her pail with 43. How many more pebbles than Dave did Gabby have?

 pebbles

$\times \div \% = \$ + ? - \times \div \% = \$? + - \% \times \div = \$ + ? - \times \div \%$

Learn to solve problems by regrouping and subtracting.

Solve these problems. Show your work in the box.
The first one has been done for you.

Laura and Max helped Aunt Molly at
her farm. They picked 58 apples and
39 pears. How many more apples than
pears did they pick?

apples

Aunt Molly made pies to sell at a local
stand. She made 32 apple pies and sold
16 of them. How many apple pies were
not sold?

pies

Laura and Max baked 24 chocolate
brownies to sell. They put frosting
on 15 of them. How many brownies
didn't have frosting?

brownies

Aunt Molly made 32 liters of apple juice.
She sold 14 liters. Aunt Molly and the
children then drank 1 liter. How many
liters of juice were left?

liters

Aunt Molly packed 15 baskets of
apples and pears and sold six of them.
How many baskets were not sold?

baskets

★ Mental Math

Learn to add and subtract quickly in your head.

Solve each problem. Figure out the answer as fast as you can in your head.

9 + 7 = [ ]   70 − 20 = [ ]   15 + 10 = [ ]

2 + 6 = [ ]   15 − 9 = [ ]   14 − 2 = [ ]

Read each problem and figure out the answer.

A pencil costs 20 ¢. Max paid for it with a quarter. How much change should Max get back?

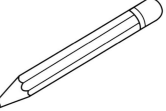

[ ]

Lucy is 11 years old. Her sister is eight. How much older is Lucy?

[ ] years

One evening, Gilbert saw five birds in the neighborhood park. Jake saw a flock of 23 birds. How many birds did they see in all?

[ ] birds

Jennifer added two cups of milk to a recipe for vanilla pudding. Then she added two more. How many cups of milk did she add in total?

[ ] cups

Learn to identify the value of numbers quickly in your head.

Look at each problem below. Write the symbol for equals (=),
is more than (>), or is less than (<) to compare the numbers.

346	◯	980		72 + 9	◯	82
14 + 6	◯	25		14 − 6	◯	8
606	◯	589		875	◯	857
25 + 5	◯	30		66 − 11	◯	55
35 − 25	◯	10		85 + 12	◯	97
8 + 10	◯	17		41 − 2	◯	39
17 − 8	◯	9		54	◯	49
25 + 25	◯	50		43 + 35	◯	78

Write the symbols for plus (+) or minus (−) to complete
each number sentence.

3 ◯ 20 = 23	90 ◯ 15 = 75	100 ◯ 20 = 80
4 ◯ 7 = 11	20 ◯ 2 = 18	5 ◯ 100 = 105
30 ◯ 20 = 50	50 ◯ 20 = 30	7 ◯ 101 = 108

★ Regroup and Add

Practice adding two-digit numbers by regrouping.

Solve these problems. Show your work in the box.
The first one has been done for you.

In a reading contest at school, Luke read
26 pages and Margo read 27 pages. How
many pages did Luke and Margo read
in all?

53

pages

```
    1
   26
 + 27
 ____
   53
```

During the last week, Jack's dad drove
48 miles in the family car and his mom
drove 46 miles in it. How many miles in
total is that?

miles

Two students decided to collect and
recycle paper. One student collected
57 pounds of paper. The other student
collected 38 pounds of paper. How
many pounds of paper did both
students collect altogether?

pounds

At Hillcrest Day School, there are 32
students in kindergarten, 27 students
in first grade, and 36 students in second
grade. How many students make up
the three grades?

students

Practice subtracting two-digit numbers by regrouping.

Solve these problems. Show your work in the box.
The first one has been done for you.

Students at Parkside School went to an amusement park. While there, 50 children went on the Ferris wheel and 47 children rode the roller coaster. How many more children went on the Ferris wheel than rode the roller coaster?

3 children

$$
\begin{array}{r}
4\ 1 \\
\cancel{5}0 \\
-\ \ 47 \\
\hline
3
\end{array}
$$

At lunchtime, 36 children met in the picnic area. Of them, 18 children went off to buy lunch. How many children were left in the picnic area?

children

After lunch, 57 children wanted to go on the water slide. Of them, 28 had already bought tickets for it. How many children still needed to buy tickets?

children

On the way back, all 97 children had to get on school buses. If 58 children had already boarded the buses, how many children still needed to get on?

children

GOAL

Practice adding and subtracting using regrouping.

Solve these problems. Show your work in the box.

Some children at Mayfair Academy were preparing for a play. Mr. Gold needed 25 yards of blue fabric and 68 yards of black fabric to make costumes for the play. How many yards did he need in all?

_____ yards

Layla bought 32 gold buttons and 28 silver buttons for the costumes. How many buttons was that in all?

_____ buttons

Mr. Walker set up a refreshment stand. He filled a basket with 75 snacks but needed a total of 105 snacks. How many more snacks did he still need?

_____ snacks

Kim and Isaac helped to set up the chairs. They already had 107 chairs but needed 67 more. How many chairs is that in total?

_____ chairs

The students sold 154 tickets for the play. The teachers sold 138. How many more tickets did the students sell than the teachers?

_____ tickets

GOAL

Identify and understand sequences or patterns of numbers.

Fill in the numbers to complete the pattern in each row.

| 2 | 4 | ☐ | 8 | 10 | ☐ | 14 | 16 | ☐ | ☐ |

| 4 | 8 | ☐ | 16 | ☐ | 24 | ☐ | 32 | ☐ | ☐ |

| 3 | ☐ | 9 | 12 | ☐ | 18 | ☐ | 24 | 27 | ☐ |

| 5 | 10 | ☐ | 20 | ☐ | 30 | 35 | ☐ | 45 | 50 |

| 105 | ☐ | 115 | 120 | ☐ | 130 | 135 | ☐ | 145 | 150 |

| 100 | ☐ | 300 | 400 | ☐ | ☐ | 700 | ☐ | 900 | 1,000 |

Find the pattern and write the missing numbers in the boxes.
Then write the number you added or subtracted to find the pattern.

| 19 | 21 | ☐ | 25 | 27 | ☐ | 31 | 33 | ☐ | ☐ |

Added ☐

| 98 | ☐ | 78 | 68 | ☐ | 48 | ☐ | 28 | ☐ | 8 |

Subtracted ☐

GOAL Learn all the combinations in a number family.

Complete the number family in each box. The first one has been done for you. **Hint:** Look for the pattern.

5 + 6 = 11	5 + 7 = 12	6 + 7 = 13
6 + 5 = 11		
11 − 6 = 5		
11 − 5 = 6		

6 + 8 = 14	6 + 9 = 15	7 + 9 = 16

3 + 4 = 7	3 + 5 = 8	9 + 8 = 17

Practice writing all the combinations in a number family.

Complete the number family in each box.

2 + 4 = 6	2 + 5 = 7	4 + 9 = 13

3 + 7 = 10	5 + 8 = 13	3 + 6 = 9

8 + 3 = 11	8 + 7 = 15	9 + 5 = 14

Mixed Problems

Practice solving problems using addition and subtraction.

Read each problem and figure out the answer.

In a basketball game, Jeff got five shots in the basket by halftime. In the second half of the game, he got four more shots in the basket. How many shots in total did Jeff get in the basket during the game?

☐ + ☐ = ☐ shots

Jessica made six apple pies for the school bake sale. She also made three more pies for her friends and two more for herself. How many pies did Jessica bake altogether?

☐ + ☐ + ☐ = ☐ pies

Mrs. Miller is driving to the airport, which is 32 miles from her house. She has already driven 21 miles. How many more miles must Mrs. Miller drive to get to the airport?

☐ − ☐ = ☐ miles

Cora and Anthony help Mr. Wright set up the classroom for a math bee. They need to set up 25 desks altogether. Mr. Wright sets up 12 desks. How many desks do Cora and Anthony set up?

☐ − ☐ = ☐ desks

Peter and Jake went to the park to play soccer. They were joined by six of their friends. How many friends played soccer together in the park?

☐ + ☐ = ☐ friends

$x ÷ % = $ + ? — x ÷ % = $? + — % x ÷ = $ + ? — x ÷ %

Practice solving problems using addition and subtraction.

Read each problem and figure out the answer.

Aidan and Kate decided to meet at the library. Aidan lives four blocks away from the library. Kate lives two blocks further from the library than Aidan. How many blocks away from the library does Kate live?

[   ] + [   ] = [   ] blocks

Kate found two books she wanted to borrow. Aidan also found two books, but then decided to put one of them back on the shelf. How many books did Kate and Aidan borrow altogether?

[   ] + [   ] − [   ] = [   ] books

Betsy and her friend Paul also went to the library. Betsy settled in a quiet corner to read her book. She read ten pages every hour. How many pages did she read in three hours?

[   ] + [   ] + [   ] = [   ] pages

Aidan, Kate, Betsy, and Paul each bought a snack at the corner store. Two of the snacks cost $2 each, and the other two cost $1 each. How much did they spend altogether?

[   ] + [   ] + [   ] + [   ] = [   ]

Aidan, Kate, and Betsy took a bus home. Kate's bus fare was $4. Aidan and Betsy each paid a dollar less than Kate. How much was Aidan's and Betsy's fare?

[   ] − [   ] = [   ]

GOAL

Learn the months and the order in which they occur.

There are 12 months in a year. Look at the months in the box.
Write them in the correct order below.

January	April	June	February
November	August	March	September
October	May	July	December

....

....

....

....

....

In which month were you born?   ....

Which month is it now?   ....

Which is the only month that begins
with the letter D?   ....

Which month comes after August?   ....

Which two months contain five letters?   ....

Months, Weeks, and Days

Learn to use a calendar.

Look at the calendar below. Then answer the questions that follow.

April

Sunday	Monday	Tuesday	Wednesday	Thursday	Friday	Saturday
			1	2	3	4
5	6	7	8	9	10	11
12	13	14	15	16	17	18
19	20	21	22	23	24	25
26	27	28	29	30		

How many days are there in April? ⬚ days

How many days are there in a week? ⬚ days

Which day is the first in a week? ....

What is the date five days after April 10? ....

What is the date on the fourth Wednesday in April? ....

What is the date one week after April 21? ....

April 1 is April Fools' Day. Which day of the week is it? ....

★ Time Problems

GOAL

Learn to tell
the time on
a clock.

 2:15

When the minute hand
points to 3, it is quarter
past or 15 minutes past.

 2:45

When the minute hand points
to 9, it is quarter to or
15 minutes to the hour.

Draw a line from each sentence to the correct matching clock.

Jack eats breakfast at 7:30 AM.

He catches the bus at 7:45 AM.

He arrives at school at 8:15 AM.

Draw the hour hand and minute hand on each clock to show the time.

Isaac goes home at 1:15.

Jane meets Ashley at quarter to two.

The baseball game begins at 6:15.

$× ÷ % = $+ ? — × ÷ % = $? + — % × ÷ = $ + ? — × ÷ %

Time Problems

Learn to tell the time with "AM" and "PM."

Read each problem and circle the correct answer.

Amy and Melissa went to a swim meet on Saturday. They arrived at the pool at 9:00 AM. The race they were competing in began 90 minutes later. What time did the race begin?

9:15 AM   10:00 AM   10:30 AM

Amy and Melissa left the pool at 11:00 AM. They went to the café for lunch at 1:00 PM. They stayed there for 45 minutes. What time did they finish?

11:45 AM   1:45 PM   2:30 PM

They were very tired when they reached home and dozed off at 2:00 PM. They woke up after 1 hour and 15 minutes. What time did they wake up?

2:15 PM   3:00 PM   3:15 PM

They went out for dinner at 6:00 PM. How many hours had passed since Amy and Melissa arrived at the swim meet?

9 hours   10 hours   11 hours

Melissa spent the night at Amy's house. They fell asleep at 8:00 PM and woke up 11 hours later. What time did they wake up?

6:00 AM   7:00 AM   9:00 PM

Amy and her dad drove Melissa home four hours after the girls woke up. What time did they drive her home?

10:00 AM   12:00 PM   11:00 AM

GOAL

Practice solving problems involving time.

Solve each problem and write the time.
Then draw hands on the clock to show the correct time.

Herman met his friends at 9:00 AM to play basketball.
They played for one hour. Then they had a break for
15 minutes and played for another 45 minutes. After
that, they left for home. What time did they leave?

11:00

tim

9:00   9:45   10:00
× 45   + 15   +1:00
9:45   10:00   11:00

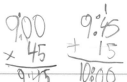 Margo takes tennis lessons. Each time, she stretches for
five minutes and plays tennis for 45 minutes. The trip
home takes ten minutes. She reaches home at 11:00 AM.
What time does her tennis lesson begin?

11:00   10:50
− 10   − 50
10:50   10:00

Kip played guitar at a talent show. He reached the town
hall at 5:30 PM and rehearsed for 15 minutes. The show
lasted 45 minutes. Then he spent 30 minutes at the
refreshment stand and left. What time did Kip leave
the town hall?

Allie takes violin lessons for 30 minutes every Thursday.
Her trip home takes 30 minutes. If she gets home at
6:00 PM, what time does her lesson begin?

Learn to read a time schedule.

Aunt Kay took Nick and Bonnie to the Springfield Toy Show.
Read the train schedule and figure out the answer to each problem.

To Springfield City

From Madison	Greenport	Springfield City
8:00 AM	8:45 AM	9:30 AM
9:00 AM	9:45 AM	10:30 AM
10:00 AM	10:45 AM	11:30 AM

To Madison

From Springfield City	Greenport	Madison
2:00 PM	2:45 PM	3:30 PM
3:00 PM	3:45 PM	4:30 PM
4:00 PM	4:45 PM	5:30 PM

The show opened at 11:00 AM. Which train did they take from
Madison to get to Springfield City 30 minutes before the opening?

What time did the train stop at Greenport on their way
to Springfield City?

The toy show ended at 3:30 PM. Which train did they take
to return home?

If they took the 4:00 PM train back home, what time did they
arrive in Madison?

GOAL

Learn to identify the value of different coins.

1¢  Penny   5¢ Nickel   10¢ Dime   25¢  Quarter

Write the value of each group of coins below.

     [ ]

[ ]

Circle the correct amount of money made up by these coins.

$1.40 $1.20 $1.35

Circle the group of coins that is worth $1.

Learn to solve problems involving money.

Nina, Lisa, Harry, and Fernando went out for lunch with their dad. Look at the restaurant's menu and then figure out the answers.

Specials at Larry's Lunch Bunch

Cheese sandwich $2.50

Macaroni and cheese $2.85

Chicken fingers $3.25

Turkey taco $3.50

Veggie burger $3.00

Fries $1.50

All drinks $1.00

Dad ordered a cheese sandwich with fries and a drink. How much did his lunch cost?

Nina ordered chicken fingers, fries, and a drink. How much did her lunch cost?

Lisa ordered one of the specials along with fries. Her lunch cost $4. Which special did she order?

Harry had $5 to buy lunch. He ordered macaroni and cheese. How much money did he have left?

Fernando ordered a turkey taco, fries, and a drink. How much did his lunch cost?

How much did everyone's lunch cost in total?

$\$ \times \div \% = \$ + ? - \times \div \% = \$? + - \% \times \div = \$ + ? - \times \div \%$

Shapes and Lines

Recognize two-dimensional (2-D) and three-dimensional (3-D) shapes.

Draw a line to match each 2-D shape to its name.

Triangle	Rectangle	Pentagon	Circle	Square

Draw a line to match each 3-D shape to its name.

  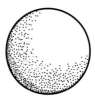  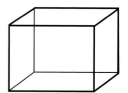

Cone	Sphere	Cube	Rectangular prism	Cylinder

Read each problem and circle the correct answer.

Which of these shapes has vertical lines?	Circle	Rectangle
Which of these shapes has diagonal lines?	Triangle	Square
How many faces does a cube have?	Four	Six
Which of these shapes does not have edges?	Sphere	Rectangular prism

$×÷%＝$+?—×÷%＝$?+—%×÷＝$+?—×÷%

Learn to identify basic fractions.

Read each problem and figure out the answer.

 This circle is cut into two equal parts. Each part is called a half. What is the fraction for a half?

 This circle is cut into four equal parts. These parts are called quarters. What is the fraction for a quarter?

 This square is cut into three equal parts. These parts are called thirds. What is the fraction for a third?

Look at each shape below. Then write the fraction that each shaded portion shows.

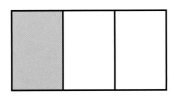 

GOAL

Learn to measure length in inches and centimeters.

Harry and Sally went fishing together. Use a ruler to measure what they found. Then write the answers to the nearest centimeter or inch in the boxes.

Harry had a worm for bait. He measured the worm.

It was ⬚ centimeters long.

A ladybug flew onto Harry's arm. Sally measured it.

It was ⬚ centimeters long.

After a long wait, Sally finally caught a fish. She measured it.

It was ⬚ inches long.

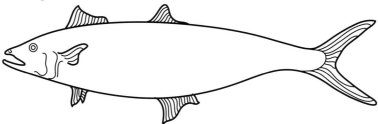

Harry caught a bigger fish than Sally. He measured it.

It was ⬚ inches long.

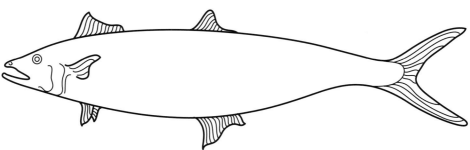

$ × ÷ % = $ + ? − × ÷ % = $? + − % × ÷ = $ + ? − × ÷ %

Practice measuring length in inches and centimeters.

Mary bought two ribbons. How long is each one?
Measure them using a ruler and give your answer in inches.

inches

inches

How long are the two pieces of ribbon altogether? ⬚ = ◯ inches

Josh picked up some leaves in the park. How long are they?
Measure them using a ruler and give your answer in centimeters.

centimeters

centimeters

How much longer is one leaf than the other? ⬚ = ◯ centimeters

Anna has a piece of rope. How long is it? Use a ruler
to measure it and give your answer in centimeters.

◯ centimeters

Can she make two equal length pieces from this piece of rope? ....

How long would each piece be? ◯ centimeters

★ Tally Marks

Learn to make tally marks on a graph to record the number of single items or groups of five items.

Kevin went hiking with his parents. He collected leaves along the trail and noted each type he found. He collected five oak leaves, eight hickory leaves, 19 dogwood leaves, 28 poplar leaves, and 35 ginkgo leaves. Make tally marks on the graph below to show the number of leaves collected. The first one has been done for you.

| = 1 leaf

┼┼┼ = 5 leaves

Leaves Collected by Kevin

Type of Leaf	Number of Leaves
Oak	┼┼┼
Hickory	
Dogwood	
Poplar	
Ginkgo	

Look carefully at the tally marks above to answer these questions.

How many oak leaves did Kevin collect? ⬚ leaves

How many more dogwood than hickory leaves did he collect? ⬚ leaves

Which leaves are 15 + 4 in number? ....

Which leaves are 30 + 5 in number? ....

Which leaves are 23 more in number than oak leaves? ....

GOAL

Reinforce understanding of tally marks on graphs.

The children in Ms. Garcia's class went on a field trip to the beach. Each child collected shells. Ellen collected six shells, Jack collected nine, Augie collected 12, and Joseph collected 15. Use tally marks to show how many shells each child collected. The first one has been done for you.

| = 1 shell

卌 = 5 shells

Shells Collected by Children

Child	Number of Shells
Ellen	卌	
Jack	
Augie	
Joseph	

Look carefully at the tally marks above to answer these questions.

Who collected the most shells? ....

Which two children collected a total of 15 shells? ....

Which child collected twice as many shells as Ellen? ....

Which child collected three more shells than Augie? ....

Which two children collected 27 shells altogether? ....

What was the total number of shells collected? ⬚ shells

★ Bar Graphs

GOAL Learn to understand the information shown on a bar graph.

Mr. Reed asked his students about the types of books they read last summer. He made a bar graph to show which types they liked best.

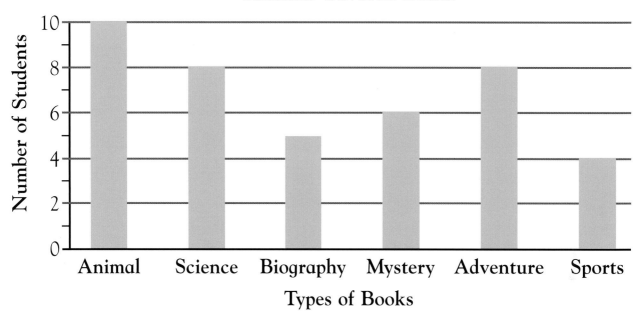

Look carefully at the bar graph above to answer these questions.

Which type of books received the fewest votes?

....

Which type of books received the same number of votes as science books?

....

Which type of books received more votes than sports but fewer than mystery?

....

Which two types of books received a total of 15 votes?

....

$×÷%=$+?−×÷%=$?+−%×÷=$+?−×÷%

Learn to understand the information shown on a picture graph.

The students in Ms. Franco's class voted for their favorite yogurt flavors. She made a graph to show the results.

Students' Favorite Yogurt Flavors 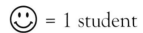 = 1 student

Type of Yogurt	Number of Students
Blueberry	☺☺☺☺☺☺☺☺☺
Strawberry	☺☺☺☺☺☺
Peach	☺☺☺☺☺☺☺☺
Banana	☺☺☺☺☺☺☺☺
Vanilla	☺☺☺☺☺☺☺☺☺☺☺☺☺☺☺☺☺

Look carefully at the picture graph above to answer these questions.

How many students voted for blueberry? ⬚ students

How many students voted for vanilla? ⬚ students

How many more votes than blueberry did vanilla receive? ⬚ students

Which two flavors received an equal number of votes? ....

Which flavor received the fewest votes? ....

Which flavor received the most votes? ....

★ More Picture Graphs

Learn to record information on a picture graph.

Ms. Green's students voted for their favorite vegetable. Ten students voted for corn, eight for cucumber, five for carrot, five for peas, and three for broccoli. Draw a picture graph to show the results. Create a key, give each column a heading, and give your graph a title.

Look carefully at your graph to answer these questions.

Which vegetable received the most number of votes? ....

Which two vegetables received ten votes in total? ....

How many students in all voted? ( ) students

$×÷%=$+?−×÷%=$?+−%×÷=$+?−×÷%

More Picture Graphs

> Reinforce your understanding of picture graphs.

Mr. Sanjay asked his students to raise their hands to vote for their favorite subjects. He made a graph to show the results.

Students' Favorite Subjects

🖐 = 1 vote

Subject	Number of Votes
Math	🖐 🖐 🖐 🖐 🖐 🖐
Science	🖐 🖐 🖐 🖐 🖐 🖐
Language Arts	🖐 🖐 🖐 🖐 🖐
Social Studies	🖐 🖐 🖐 🖐

Look carefully at the graph to answer these questions.

Which subjects received the same number of votes? ....

Which subject received fewer votes than language arts? ....

How many students voted for math? ⬜ students

How many students voted for social studies? ⬜ students

How many more students voted for math than social studies? ⬜ students

Certificate

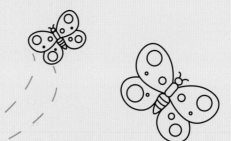

2nd Grade

Congratulations to

....

for successfully finishing this book.

GOOD JOB!

You're a star.

Date

....

Answer Section with Parents' Notes

This book is intended to teach math problem solving to second grade children. The content is designed to feature problems similar to those they may encounter in everyday life.

Contents
By working through this book, your child will practice:
- using number lines to add and subtract;
- solving "mental math" problems without writing them down;
- adding and subtracting two- and three-digit numbers by regrouping;
- identifying number patterns and families;
- reading math terms and identifying key words and phrases in word problems;
- identifying place value—hundreds, tens, and ones;
- recognizing even and odd numbers;
- solving problems related to money;
- using a calendar and telling the time to solve problems;
- solving measurement problems;
- learning shapes and simple fractions;
- interpreting data from graphs and creating graphs to solve problems.

How to Help Your Child
Guide your child by reading the problems and instructions slowly. Make sure he or she understands the questions, the concepts involved, and the different math terms being used.

As you work with your child, you will get an idea of what he or she finds easy, as well as what is more challenging. Use a hands-on approach to help your child understand any concepts he or she finds difficult to grasp. For example, use blocks or other objects found around the home to practice counting, adding, and multiplying. It may also be useful to have a small notebook or chalkboard to jot down numbers and to draw on.

Remember to build your child's confidence by praising success. Encourage your child to persist when faced with small challenges. Always remember that finding solutions to math problems should be exciting.

★ Number Lines

GOAL Learn to use a number line to add and subtract.

Use the number line to add or subtract. Write the number sentence you use and then the answer. The first one has been done for you.

Stacy planted 13 tomato plants. Barry planted seven lettuce plants. How many plants did they plant in all?

10 11 12 13 14 15 16 17 18 19 20

[13 + 7 = 20]   [20] plants

On Monday, it snowed 6 inches in the town of Millbrook. On Tuesday, it snowed 7 inches. How much snow fell in those two days?

0 1 2 3 4 5 6 7 8 9 10 11 12 13

[6 + 7 = 13]   [13] inches

There were 36 birds in a tree. After a while, three birds flew away. How many birds were left in the tree?

30 31 32 33 34 35 36 37 38 39 40

[36 – 3 = 33]   [33] birds

Nicole collected 15 coins and Gary collected nine. How many more coins than Gary has Nicole collected?

5 6 7 8 9 10 11 12 13 14 15

[15 – 9 = 6]   [6] coins

Number lines provide a visual aid for addition and subtraction problems. They demonstrate how to count up when adding and count down when subtracting.

Number Words ★

GOAL Learn to recognize numbers when they are written as words.

Find the number words from the box in the word search.

one	three	four	two	six
hundred	seventeen	forty-five
fifty	ninety	twelve	seventy	thirty

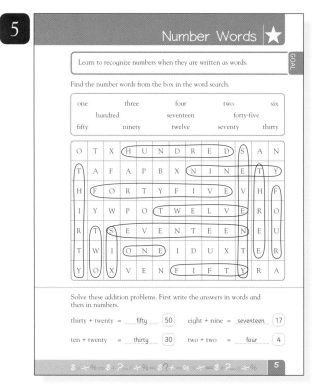

Solve these addition problems. First write the answers in words and then in numbers.

thirty + twenty = _fifty_ [50]   eight + nine = _seventeen_ [17]

ten + twenty = _thirty_ [30]   two + two = _four_ [4]

It is important for your child to recognize the word forms of numbers. He or she will feel more confident when reading word problems that include number words.

★ Number Words

GOAL Practice recognizing numbers when they are written as words.

Draw a line to match the number on the left to the correct number word on the right.

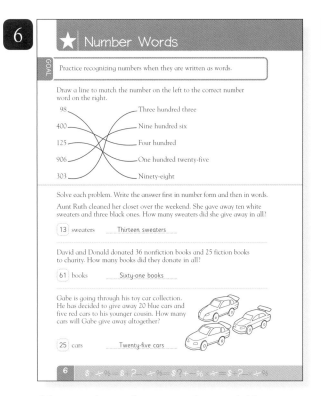

98 — Three hundred three
400 — Nine hundred six
125 — Four hundred
906 — One hundred twenty-five
303 — Ninety-eight

Solve each problem. Write the answer first in number form and then in words.

Aunt Ruth cleaned her closet over the weekend. She gave away ten white sweaters and three black ones. How many sweaters did she give away in all?

[13] sweaters   Thirteen sweaters

David and Donald donated 36 nonfiction books and 25 fiction books to charity. How many books did they donate in all?

[61] books   Sixty-one books

Gabe is going through his toy car collection. He has decided to give away 20 blue cars and five red cars to his younger cousin. How many cars will Gabe give away altogether?

[25] cars   Twenty-five cars

After completing this page with your child, play a game of matching 20 cards with numbers (numerals) written on them with 20 cards with corresponding number words on them to reinforce word recognition.

Math Terms ★

GOAL Learn the terms "addends" and "sums" used in addition. Addends are numbers added together to equal a sum.

Write the addend that's missing from each number sentence.

1 + [9] = 10   [9] + 1 = 10   5 + [5] = 10

3 + [7] = 10   [7] + 3 = 10   6 + [4] = 10

2 + [8] = 10   [4] + 6 = 10   [8] + 2 = 10

Find the sum for each problem.

15 + 2 = [17]   2 + 12 = [14]   13 + 7 = [20]

8 + 3 = [11]   7 + 5 = [12]   11 + 9 = [20]

Read the story below and circle all the numbers of fruits mentioned in it.

Mark and Fiona went to the supermarket. They wanted to buy different kinds of fruit. They bought ④apples and ⑥bananas and put them in a bag. Next Mark and Fiona looked for other fruit. They bought ⑥pears, ④oranges, and ②plums. Then they went home to make fresh fruit salad!

Now write the numbers you circled in the boxes below. Finally, add them to find the sum, or the total number of fruits.

[4] apples + [6] bananas + [6] pears + [4] oranges + [2] plums

= [22] fruits

Explain to your child the meaning of the terms "addend" and "sum" (or "total") in addition problems. These are the key math terms to know.

★ Math Terms

Learn the words often used in math problems.

Use words from the word box to complete the crossword puzzle below.

| ten | plus | number line | equal | minus | digit | total |

Across

1. A line sometimes used to add or subtract
2. The number 12 is a two-_____ number
7. Word for the symbol **+**

Down

3. Word for the symbol **–**
4. Another word for **sum**
5. Word for 10
6. Word for the symbol **=**

Crossword puzzle:
- 4 down: t o t a l
- 3 down: m n s
- 2 across: d i g i t
- 1 across: n u m b e r l i n e
- 5 down: t e n
- 6 down: e q u a l
- 7 across: p l u s

Solving a crossword puzzle is a challenging but enjoyable way for your child to learn math terms and their meanings. Learning math terms will help him or her solve word problems, understand math concepts and operations, and become fluent in discussing problems.

Add Up to 20 ★

Learn to solve problems that involve adding up to 20.

Solve these problems. First write the number sentence you use, then write the answer. The first one has been done for you.

Jack has a collection of rocks. He has 14 black rocks and four gray rocks. How many rocks does Jack have altogether?

$14 + 4 = 18$ | 18 rocks

Lola baked cupcakes for her classmates. She baked eight chocolate cupcakes and six vanilla ones. How many cupcakes did Lola bake altogether?

$8 + 6 = 14$ | 14 cupcakes

Pam has five history books and 12 science books on her bookshelf. How many books for both subjects does Pam have?

$5 + 12 = 17$ | 17 books

Tim and Andre are playing with their toy cars. Tim has eight cars, and Andre has 11 cars. How many toy cars do they have in all?

$8 + 11 = 19$ | 19 cars

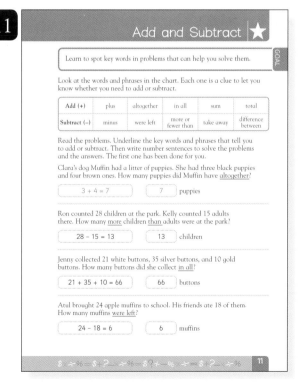

When your child begins to solve word problems, he or she may need to refer to pictures or symbols of the objects she is counting, adding, or subtracting. Let him or her use the pictures for help. Soon your child will be able to solve problems using only numbers.

★ Subtract Two-Digit Numbers

Learn to solve problems that involve subtracting two-digit numbers.

Figure out each answer. Write the number sentence you use and then the answer. The first one has been done for you.

A school garden has 15 plants. Mason watered 10 of them. How many more plants does he still have to water?

$15 - 10 = 5$ | 5 plants

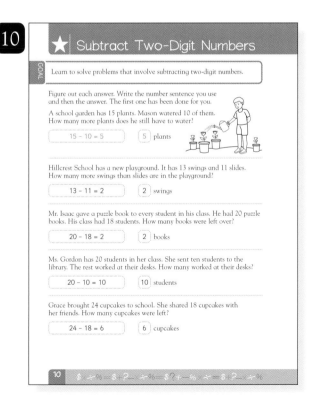

Hillcrest School has a new playground. It has 13 swings and 11 slides. How many more swings than slides are in the playground?

$13 - 11 = 2$ | 2 swings

Mr. Isaac gave a puzzle book to every student in his class. He had 20 puzzle books. His class had 18 students. How many books were left over?

$20 - 18 = 2$ | 2 books

Ms. Gordon has 20 students in her class. She sent ten students to the library. The rest worked at their desks. How many worked at their desks?

$20 - 10 = 10$ | 10 students

Grace brought 24 cupcakes to school. She shared 18 cupcakes with her friends. How many cupcakes were left?

$24 - 18 = 6$ | 6 cupcakes

As you introduce subtraction problems to your child, use objects or pictures of objects and the words "minus" or "take away" to show how it works. Remove or draw a line through the number of objects being taken away.

Add and Subtract ★

Learn to spot key words in problems that can help you solve them.

Look at the words and phrases in the chart. Each one is a clue to let you know whether you need to add or subtract.

Add (+)	plus	altogether	in all	sum	total
Subtract (–)	minus	were left	more or fewer than	take away	difference between

Read the problems. Underline the key words and phrases that tell you to add or subtract. Then write number sentences to solve the problems and the answers. The first one has been done for you.

Clara's dog Muffin had a litter of puppies. She had three black puppies and four brown ones. How many puppies did Muffin have <u>altogether</u>?

$3 + 4 = 7$ | 7 puppies

Ron counted 28 children at the park. Kelly counted 15 adults there. How many <u>more</u> children <u>than</u> adults were at the park?

$28 - 15 = 13$ | 13 children

Jenny collected 21 white buttons, 35 silver buttons, and 10 gold buttons. How many buttons did she collect <u>in all</u>?

$21 + 35 + 10 = 66$ | 66 buttons

Atul brought 24 apple muffins to school. His friends ate 18 of them. How many muffins <u>were left</u>?

$24 - 18 = 6$ | 6 muffins

Solving word problems can be challenging even for children who excel at math. As you read the problems, point out the key words that tell your child which operations to use in the equation.

★ Hundreds, Tens, and Ones

Learn about the place values of hundreds, tens, and ones in three-digit numbers. For example, the number 234 is made up of 2 hundreds, 3 tens, and 4 ones.

Hundreds	Tens	Ones
2	3	4

For each number, write how many hundreds, tens, and ones it has in the box below.

789
Hundreds	Tens	Ones
7	8	9

100
Hundreds	Tens	Ones
1	0	0

906
Hundreds	Tens	Ones
9	0	6

453
Hundreds	Tens	Ones
4	5	3

634
Hundreds	Tens	Ones
6	3	4

230
Hundreds	Tens	Ones
2	3	0

Choose the correct number from above to solve each riddle below.

I am the number two hundred thirty. `230`

I have no tens and no ones. `100`

I am the number closest to 1,000. `906`

I am a number greater than 453 but less than 789. `634`

I can be added to 400 and the sum will be 853. `453`

Understanding place value lays a good foundation for adding and subtracting—and, in later grades, for multiplying. It is especially useful when regrouping and carrying over in addition or borrowing in subtraction.

Hundreds, Tens, and Ones ★

Reinforce understanding of hundreds, tens, and ones (place value).

Circle the place value of the underlined digit.

6	1	6 hundreds	(6 tens)	6 ones
29	7	7 hundreds	7 tens	(7 ones)
3	00	(3 hundreds)	3 tens	3 ones
4 5 3		5 hundreds	(5 tens)	5 ones
90	7	7 hundreds	7 tens	(7 ones)

Read each problem and figure out the answer.

Subtract 2 ones from the number 356. `354`

Add 5 tens and 3 ones to the number 723. `776`

Add 2 hundreds to the number 296. `496`

Subtract 2 tens and 6 ones from 829. `803`

Add 3 hundreds, 2 tens, and 5 ones to the number 174. `499`

Give your child more practice in place value. Write down a few large numbers and ask him or her to tell you the place value of each digit. If your child is completely comfortable with hundreds, tens, and ones, consider introducing him or her to the thousands place.

★ Even and Odd Numbers

Learn to identify even and odd numbers. Even numbers end in 0, 2, 4, 6, or 8. Odd numbers end in 1, 3, 5, 7, or 9.

Count the objects in each row. Circle pairs of the objects. Are the number of objects even or odd? Circle the answer.

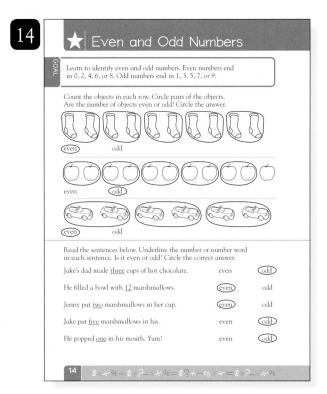

(even)   odd

even   (odd)

(even)   odd

Read the sentences below. Underline the number or number word in each sentence. Is it even or odd? Circle the correct answer.

Jake's dad made three cups of hot chocolate.   even   (odd)

He filled a bowl with 12 marshmallows.   (even)   odd

Jenny put two marshmallows in her cup.   (even)   odd

Jake put five marshmallows in his.   even   (odd)

He popped one in his mouth. Yum!   even   (odd)

Learning even and odd numbers lets your child see patterns and recognize that even numbers can be divided in two equal halves. Explore real-life examples, such as a dozen eggs or a deck of 52 cards, to find even and odd numbers and quantities.

Even and Odd Numbers ★

Practice identifying even and odd numbers.

Jim is going fishing. Help him catch the nine fish with odd numbers on them by coloring them in.

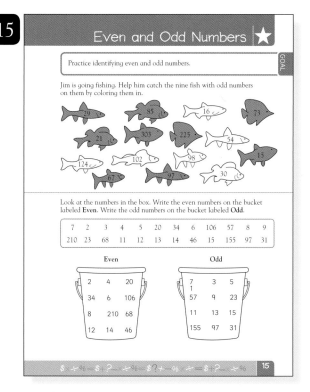

Look at the numbers in the box. Write the even numbers on the bucket labeled **Even**. Write the odd numbers on the bucket labeled **Odd**.

7	2	3	4	5	20	34	6	106	57	8	9
210	23	68	11	12	13	14	46	15	155	97	31

Even
2	4	20
34	6	106
8	210	68
12	14	46

Odd
7	3	5
1		
57	9	23
11	13	15
155	97	31

Use this page to reinforce even and odd numbers. If necessary, use small items, such as pennies, to show how an even number of items can be paired, unlike an odd number of items. Review that even numbers end in 0, 2, 4, 6, or 8 and odd numbers end in 1, 3, 5, 7, or 9.

★ Regroup and Add

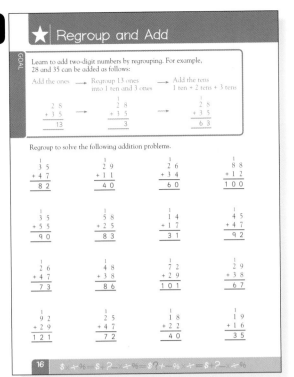

GOAL: Learn to add two-digit numbers by regrouping. For example, 28 and 35 can be added as follows:

Add the ones → Regroup 13 ones into 1 ten and 3 ones → Add the tens 1 ten + 2 tens + 3 tens

```
   2 8          1            1
 + 3 5         2 8          2 8
 ─────    →  + 3 5    →   + 3 5
  1 3         ───          ─────
               3            6 3
```

Regroup to solve the following addition problems.

```
  1             1             1             1
  3 5           2 9           2 6           8 8
+ 4 7         + 1 1         + 3 4         + 1 2
─────         ─────         ─────         ─────
  8 2           4 0           6 0         1 0 0


  1             1             1             1
  3 5           5 8           1 4           4 5
+ 5 5         + 2 5         + 1 7         + 4 7
─────         ─────         ─────         ─────
  9 0           8 3           3 1           9 2


  1             1             1             1
  2 6           4 8           7 2           2 9
+ 4 7         + 3 8         + 2 9         + 3 8
─────         ─────         ─────         ─────
  7 3           8 6         1 0 1           6 7


  1             1             1             1
  9 2           2 5           1 8           1 9
+ 2 9         + 4 7         + 2 2         + 1 6
─────         ─────         ─────         ─────
1 2 1           7 2           4 0           3 5
```

The regrouping in all of these addition problems involves carrying 1, which represents ten ones, or one ten, into the tens place value. Regrouping, or carrying, is a method of carrying a number from the ones to the tens place.

Regroup and Add ★

GOAL: Learn to solve problems by regrouping and adding.

Cara, Jeff, and their mom were waiting at the airport to board their plane. Solve these problems. Show your work in the box. The first one has been done for you.

Cara counted 16 people waiting in a line. Jeff counted 25 people sitting in chairs. How many people did they count in all?
(41) people
```
   1
   1 6
 + 2 5
 ─────
   4 1
```

Jeff counted the number of children waiting at the airport. He counted 24 boys and 28 girls. How many children did he count in all?
(52) children
```
   1
   2 4
 + 2 8
 ─────
   5 2
```

Cara counted 18 books and 28 magazines on a book stand. How many books and magazines did she count in all?
(46) books and magazines
```
   1
   1 8
 + 2 8
 ─────
   4 6
```

Jeff bought 16 fruit bars at the snack stand. Cara bought three bottles of water and three bags of pretzels. How many items did they buy altogether?
(22) items
```
16 + (3 + 3)     1
= 16 + 6        1 6
              +   6
              ─────
                2 2
```

Mom said they had waited 15 minutes. They had 35 minutes more before they could get on the plane. How long did they have to wait in total?
(50) minutes
```
   1
   1 5
 + 3 5
 ─────
   5 0
```

In some schools, regrouping may not be taught until 3rd or 4th grade. If your child is struggling, be ready to offer him or her extra guidance when working through these problems.

★ Regroup and Subtract

GOAL: Learn to subtract from two-digit numbers by regrouping.

Borrow 1 ten from the tens to make 15 ones → Subtract 6 ones from 15 → Subtract 2 tens from 3 tens

```
  3 1            3 1           3 1
  4̸ 5           4̸ 5          4̸ 5
- 2 6          - 2 6         - 2 6
─────     →    ─────    →    ─────
                   9           1 9
```

Solve these problems. Show your work in the box. The first one has been done for you.

Dave and Gabby went to the beach to build a sand castle. Dave started the castle and built it seven inches high. Gabby then increased the height to 14 inches. How much taller did Gabby make the castle?
(7) inches
```
  0 1
  1̸ 4
-   7
─────
    7
```

Gabby built eight steps going up the castle. Then Dave added more. The total number of steps was 17. How many steps did Dave build?
(9) steps
```
  0 1
  1̸ 7
-   8
─────
    9
```

Dave and Gabby made 26 little windows. Of those, Gabby made eight. How many windows did Dave make?
(18) windows
```
  1 1
  2̸ 6
-   8
─────
  1 8
```

Dave filled his pail with 37 pebbles to place around the castle. Gabby filled her pail with 43. How many more pebbles than Dave did Gabby have?
(6) pebbles
```
  3 1
  4̸ 3
- 3 7
─────
    6
```

While subtracting, explain to your child how to borrow from the tens. Review the example at the top of the page and create other examples that involve regrouping, such as 45 – 27 and 62 – 49.

Regroup and Subtract ★

GOAL: Learn to solve problems by regrouping and subtracting.

Solve these problems. Show your work in the box. The first one has been done for you.

Laura and Max helped Aunt Molly at her farm. They picked 58 apples and 39 pears. How many more apples than pears did they pick?
(19) apples
```
  4 1
  5̸ 8
- 3 9
─────
  1 9
```

Aunt Molly made pies to sell at a local stand. She made 32 apple pies and sold 16 of them. How many apple pies were not sold?
(16) pies
```
  2 1
  3̸ 2
- 1 6
─────
  1 6
```

Laura and Max baked 24 chocolate brownies to sell. They put frosting on 15 of them. How many brownies didn't have frosting?
(9) brownies
```
  1 1
  2̸ 4
- 1 5
─────
    9
```

Aunt Molly made 32 liters of apple juice. She sold 14 liters. Aunt Molly and the children drank 1 liter. How many liters of juice were left?
(17) liters
```
  2 1
  3̸ 2          1 8
- 1 4         -  1
─────         ───
  1 8          1 7
```

Aunt Molly packed 15 baskets of apples and pears and sold six of them. How many baskets were not sold?
(9) baskets
```
  0 1
  1̸ 5
-   6
─────
    9
```

"Regrouping," "borrowing," or "carrying over" in subtraction all refer to taking one set of tens and turning it into a set of ten ones. If your child has not yet covered this concept in school, these pages may prove challenging. Be patient, and offer extra support where needed.

★ Mental Math

Learn to add and subtract quickly in your head.

Solve each problem. Figure out the answer as fast as you can in your head.

9 + 7 = 16   70 − 20 = 50   15 + 10 = 25

2 + 6 = 8   15 − 9 = 6   14 − 2 = 12

Read each problem and figure out the answer.

A pencil costs 20 ¢. Max paid for it with a quarter. How much change should Max get back?

5 ¢

Lucy is 11 years old. Her sister is eight. How much older is Lucy?

3 years

One evening, Gilbert saw five birds in the neighborhood park. Jake saw a flock of 23 birds. How many birds did they see in all?

28 birds

Jennifer added two cups of milk to a recipe for vanilla pudding. Then she added two more. How many cups of milk did she add in total?

4 cups

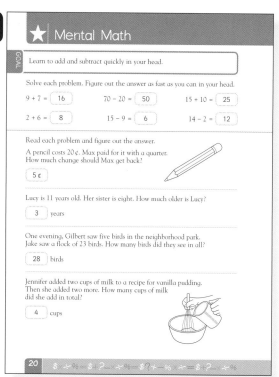

Check your child's ability to answer simple math problems without counting on his or her fingers or writing down numbers. He or she will need to gain proficiency in adding and subtracting basic numbers mentally.

Mental Math ★

Learn to identify the value of numbers quickly in your head.

Look at each problem below. Write the symbol for equals (=), is more than (>), or is less than (<) to compare the numbers.

346	<	980		72 + 9	<	82
14 + 6	<	25		14 − 6	=	8
606	>	589		875	>	857
25 + 5	=	30		66 − 11	=	55
35 − 25	=	10		85 + 12	=	97
8 + 10	>	17		41 − 2	=	39
17 − 8	=	9		54	>	49
25 + 25	=	50		43 + 35	=	78

Write the symbols for plus (+) or minus (−) to complete each number sentence.

3 + 20 = 23   90 − 15 = 75   100 − 20 = 80

4 + 7 = 11   20 − 2 = 18   5 + 100 = 105

30 + 20 = 50   50 − 20 = 30   7 + 101 = 108

Inserting the missing sign in the activities on this page makes an engaging way for your child to compare values and figure out problems in his or her head. Remind your child to work slowly and carefully.

★ Regroup and Add

Practice adding two-digit numbers by regrouping.

Solve these problems. Show your work in the box. The first one has been done for you.

In a reading contest at school, Luke read 26 pages and Margo read 27 pages. How many pages did Luke and Margo read in all?

53 pages

```
  1
  26
+ 27
  53
```

During the last week, Jack's dad drove 48 miles in the family car and his mom drove 46 miles in it. How many miles in total is that?

94 miles

```
  1
  48
+ 46
  94
```

Two students decided to collect and recycle paper. One student collected 57 pounds of paper. The other student collected 38 pounds of paper. How many pounds of paper did both students collect altogether?

95 pounds

```
  1
  57
+ 38
  95
```

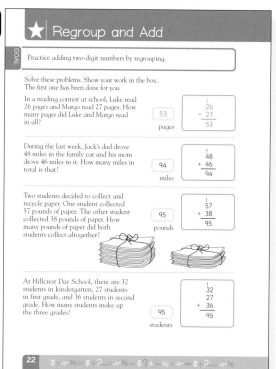

At Hillcrest Day School, there are 32 students in kindergarten, 27 students in first grade, and 36 students in second grade. How many students make up the three grades?

95 students

```
  1
  32
  27
+ 36
  95
```

When regrouping in addition, carefully explain the process to your child, using terms such as "digits," "ones column," "tens column," and "hundreds column." As you work on an addition problem, always write the number 1 at the top of the tens or hundreds column, as an aid.

Regroup and Subtract ★

Practice subtracting two-digit numbers by regrouping.

Solve these problems. Show your work in the box. The first one has been done for you.

Students at Parkside School went to an amusement park. While there, 50 children went on the Ferris wheel and 47 children rode the roller coaster. How many more children went on the Ferris wheel than rode the roller coaster?

3 children

```
  4 1
  5̶0̶
− 4 7
    3
```

At lunchtime, 36 children met in the picnic area. Of them, 18 children went off to buy lunch. How many children were left in the picnic area?

18 children

```
  2 1
  3̶6̶
− 1 8
  1 8
```

After lunch, 57 children wanted to go on the water slide. Of them, 28 had already bought tickets for it. How many children still needed to buy tickets?

29 children

```
  4 1
  5̶7̶
− 2 8
  2 9
```

On the way back, all 97 children had to get on school buses. If 58 children had already boarded the buses, how many children still needed to get on?

39 children

```
  8 1
  9̶7̶
− 5 8
  3 9
```

Teach your child how to check the answer to any subtraction problem by adding the difference (the answer) to the number that is being taken away. This will reinforce the relationship between addition and subtraction.

★ More Regrouping

GOAL Practice adding and subtracting using regrouping.

Solve these problems. Show your work in the box.

Some children at Mayfair Academy were preparing for a play. Mr. Gold needed 25 yards of blue fabric and 68 yards of black fabric to make costumes for the play. How many yards did he need in all?

93 yards

$$\begin{array}{r} 1 \\ 25 \\ + 68 \\ \hline 93 \end{array}$$

Layla bought 32 gold buttons and 28 silver buttons for the costumes. How many buttons was that in all?

60 buttons

$$\begin{array}{r} 1 \\ 32 \\ + 28 \\ \hline 60 \end{array}$$

Mr. Walker set up a refreshment stand. He filled a basket with 75 snacks but needed a total of 105 snacks. How many more snacks did he still need?

30 snacks

$$\begin{array}{r} 0\,1 \\ \cancel{105} \\ - 75 \\ \hline 30 \end{array}$$

Kim and Isaac helped to set up the chairs. They already had 107 chairs but needed 67 more. How many chairs is that in total?

174 chairs

$$\begin{array}{r} 1 \\ 107 \\ + 67 \\ \hline 174 \end{array}$$

The students sold 154 tickets for the play. The teachers sold 138. How many more tickets did the students sell than the teachers?

16 tickets

$$\begin{array}{r} 4\,1 \\ \cancel{154} \\ - 138 \\ \hline 16 \end{array}$$

Help your child solve more complicated word problems by guiding him or her through each one slowly. Read and circle key information, highlight what needs to be figured out, and determine which operation or operations are needed to solve the problem.

Number Patterns ★

GOAL Identify and understand sequences or patterns of numbers.

Fill in the numbers to complete the pattern in each row.

2   4   [6]   8   10   [12]   14   16   [18]   [20]

4   8   [12]   16   [20]   24   [28]   32   [36]   [40]

3   [6]   9   12   [15]   18   [21]   24   27   [30]

5   10   [15]   20   [25]   30   35   [40]   45   50

105   [110]   115   120   [125]   130   135   [140]   145   150

100   [200]   300   400   [500]   [600]   700   [800]   900   1,000

Find the pattern and write the missing numbers in the boxes. Then write the number you added or subtracted to find the pattern.

19   21   [23]   25   27   [29]   31   33   [35]   [37]

Added [2]

98   [88]   78   68   [58]   48   [38]   28   [18]   8

Subtracted [10]

Patterns can be numbers, shapes, objects, and other items that grow in a sequence that continues and repeats itself over and over again. Seeing a pattern can help your child solve complicated problems because they let him or her predict what will come next.

★ Number Families

GOAL Learn all the combinations in a number family.

Complete the number family in each box. The first one has been done for you. **Hint:** Look for the pattern.

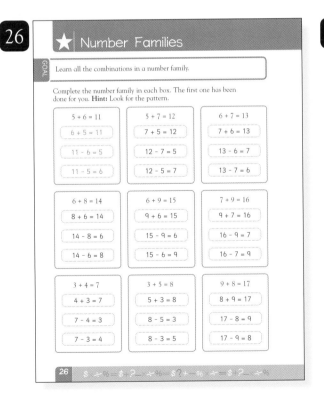

5 + 6 = 11	5 + 7 = 12	6 + 7 = 13
6 + 5 = 11	7 + 5 = 12	7 + 6 = 13
11 - 6 = 5	12 - 7 = 5	13 - 6 = 7
11 - 5 = 6	12 - 5 = 7	13 - 7 = 6

6 + 8 = 14	6 + 9 = 15	7 + 9 = 16
8 + 6 = 14	9 + 6 = 15	9 + 7 = 16
14 - 8 = 6	15 - 9 = 6	16 - 9 = 7
14 - 6 = 8	15 - 6 = 9	16 - 7 = 9

3 + 4 = 7	3 + 5 = 8	9 + 8 = 17
4 + 3 = 7	5 + 3 = 8	8 + 9 = 17
7 - 4 = 3	8 - 5 = 3	17 - 8 = 9
7 - 3 = 4	8 - 3 = 5	17 - 9 = 8

Writing out number families, like the ones on this page, should greatly improve your child's skill and speed in finding answers to math equations. In later grades, your child will likely encounter number families involving multiplication and division.

Number Families ★

GOAL Practice writing all the combinations in a number family.

Complete the number family in each box.

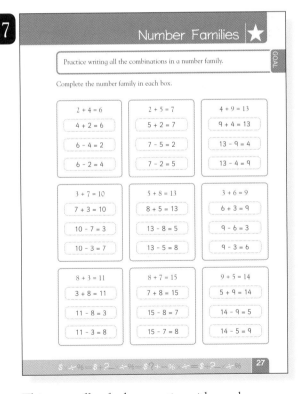

2 + 4 = 6	2 + 5 = 7	4 + 9 = 13
4 + 2 = 6	5 + 2 = 7	9 + 4 = 13
6 - 4 = 2	7 - 5 = 2	13 - 9 = 4
6 - 2 = 4	7 - 2 = 5	13 - 4 = 9

3 + 7 = 10	5 + 8 = 13	3 + 6 = 9
7 + 3 = 10	8 + 5 = 13	6 + 3 = 9
10 - 7 = 3	13 - 8 = 5	9 - 6 = 3
10 - 3 = 7	13 - 5 = 8	9 - 3 = 6

8 + 3 = 11	8 + 7 = 15	9 + 5 = 14
3 + 8 = 11	7 + 8 = 15	5 + 9 = 14
11 - 8 = 3	15 - 8 = 7	14 - 9 = 5
11 - 3 = 8	15 - 7 = 8	14 - 5 = 9

This page offers further practice with number families. You could also play a game with your child. Write six common, but tricky, addition and subtraction equations on the sides of a small square box. Then roll the box, look at the equation on the top face, and ask your child to write out another equation in its number family.

★ Mixed Problems

Practice solving problems using addition and subtraction.

Read each problem and figure out the answer.

In a basketball game, Jeff got five shots in the basket by halftime. In the second half of the game, he got four more shots in the basket. How many shots in total did Jeff get in the basket during the game?

[5] + [4] = [9] shots

Jessica made six apple pies for the school bake sale. She also made three more pies for her friends and two more for herself. How many pies did Jessica bake altogether?

[6] + [3] + [2] = [11] pies

Mrs. Miller is driving to the airport, which is 32 miles from her house. She has already driven 21 miles. How many more miles must Mrs. Miller drive to get to the airport?

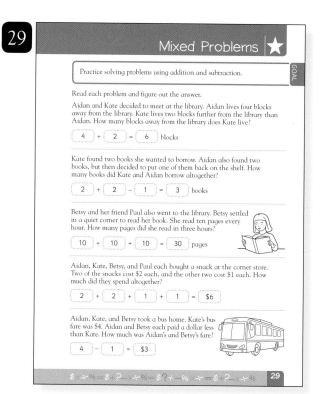

[32] − [21] = [11] miles

Cora and Anthony help Mr. Wright set up the classroom for a math bee. They need to set up 25 desks altogether. Mr. Wright sets up 12 desks. How many desks do Cora and Anthony set up?

[25] − [12] = [13] desks

Peter and Jake went to the park to play soccer. They were joined by six of their friends. How many friends played soccer together in the park?

[2] + [6] = [8] friends

Working through the problems on this page and the next will help reinforce the problem-solving skills that your child has learned so far. Before your child starts, it might be useful to review the previous activities in the book with him or her—particularly the pages on regrouping and key words to look out for in math problems.

Mixed Problems ★

Practice solving problems using addition and subtraction.

Read each problem and figure out the answer.

Aidan and Kate decided to meet at the library. Aidan lives four blocks away from the library. Kate lives two blocks further from the library than Aidan. How many blocks away from the library does Kate live?

[4] + [2] = [6] blocks

Kate found two books she wanted to borrow. Aidan also found two books, but then decided to put one of them back on the shelf. How many books did Kate and Aidan borrow altogether?

[2] + [2] − [1] = [3] books

Betsy and her friend Paul also went to the library. Betsy settled in a quiet corner to read her book. She read ten pages every hour. How many pages did she read in three hours?

[10] + [10] + [10] = [30] pages

Aidan, Kate, Betsy, and Paul each bought a snack at the corner store. Two of the snacks cost $2 each, and the other two cost $1 each. How much did they spend altogether?

[2] + [2] + [1] + [1] = [$6]

Aidan, Kate, and Betsy took a bus home. Kate's bus fare was $4. Aidan and Betsy each paid a dollar less than Kate. How much was Aidan's and Betsy's fare?

[4] − [1] = [$3]

Successfully completing this page and the previous one should give your child a solid foundation for tackling the more challenging math problems that he or she will encounter in higher grades.

★ Months of the Year

Learn the months and the order in which they occur.

There are 12 months in a year. Look at the months in the box. Write them in the correct order below.

January	April	June	February
November	August	March	September
October	May	July	December

January	July
February	August
March	September
April	October
May	November
June	December

In which month were you born? **Answers may vary**

Which month is it now? **Answers may vary**

Which is the only month that begins with the letter D? December

Which month comes after August? September

Which two months contain five letters? April and March

Your child should know the names, spellings, and order of the months. Use this page along with a calendar to teach your child the months, as well as ordinal numbers—first (1st), second (2nd), third (3rd), and so on—which we use when saying dates aloud.

Months, Weeks, and Days ★

Learn to use a calendar.

Look at the calendar below. Then answer the questions that follow.

April

Sunday	Monday	Tuesday	Wednesday	Thursday	Friday	Saturday
			1	2	3	4
5	6	7	8	9	10	11
12	13	14	15	16	17	18
19	20	21	22	23	24	25
26	27	28	29	30		

How many days are there in April? [30] days

How many days are there in a week? [7] days

Which day is the first in a week? Sunday

What is the date five days after April 10? April 15

What is the date on the fourth Wednesday in April? April 22

What is the date one week after April 21? April 28

April 1 is April Fools' Day. Which day of the week is it? Wednesday

If you have a calendar in your home, review it with your child. Point out important dates, such as school and family events and birthdays. Incorporating checking the calendar into your child's daily routine will improve his or her confidence with months and dates.

★ Time Problems

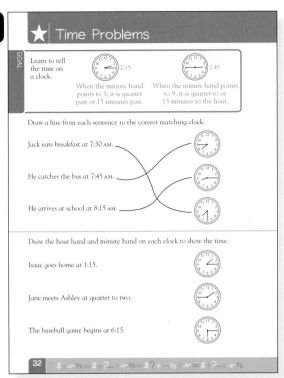

GOAL Learn to tell the time on a clock.

2:15
When the minute hand points to 3, it is quarter past or 15 minutes past.

2:45
When the minute hand points to 9, it is quarter to or 15 minutes to the hour.

Draw a line from each sentence to the correct matching clock.

Jack eats breakfast at 7:30 AM.

He catches the bus at 7:45 AM.

He arrives at school at 8:15 AM.

Draw the hour hand and minute hand on each clock to show the time.

Isaac goes home at 1:15.

Jane meets Ashley at quarter to two.

The baseball game begins at 6:15.

Use a toy clock or make one from a paper plate and a short and long straw connected to the center of the plate. Turn each straw as you point and count the hours. You can also point out that 12 five-minute intervals make up a 60-minute hour.

Time Problems ★

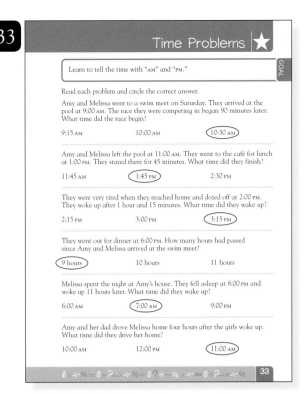

GOAL Learn to tell the time with "AM" and "PM".

Read each problem and circle the correct answer.

Amy and Melissa went to a swim meet on Saturday. They arrived at the pool at 9:00 AM. The race they were competing in began 90 minutes later. What time did the race begin?

9:15 AM   10:00 AM   (10:30 AM)

Amy and Melissa left the pool at 11:00 AM. They went to the café for lunch at 1:00 PM. They stayed there for 45 minutes. What time did they finish?

11:45 AM   (1:45 PM)   2:30 PM

They were very tired when they reached home and dozed off at 2:00 PM. They woke up after 1 hour and 15 minutes. What time did they wake up?

2:15 PM   3:00 PM   (3:15 PM)

They went out for dinner at 6:00 PM. How many hours had passed since Amy and Melissa arrived at the swim meet?

(9 hours)   10 hours   11 hours

Melissa spent the night at Amy's house. They fell asleep at 8:00 PM and woke up 11 hours later. What time did they wake up?

6:00 AM   (7:00 AM)   9:00 PM

Amy and her dad drove Melissa home four hours after the girls woke up. What time did they drive her home?

10:00 AM   12:00 PM   (11:00 AM)

Using a clock, explain to your child that a day has 24 hours. The hours from 12:00 midnight until just before 12:00 noon are called "AM" hours, or morning hours. The hours from 12:00 noon to 12:00 midnight are called "PM" hours, or afternoon and evening hours.

★ More Time Problems

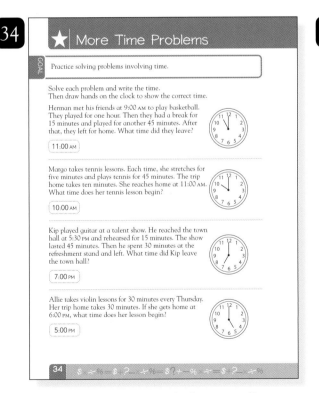

GOAL Practice solving problems involving time.

Solve each problem and write the time.
Then draw hands on the clock to show the correct time.

Herman met his friends at 9:00 AM to play basketball. They played for one hour. Then they had a break for 15 minutes and played for another 45 minutes. After that, they left for home. What time did they leave?

11:00 AM

Margo takes tennis lessons. Each time, she stretches for five minutes and plays tennis for 45 minutes. The trip home takes ten minutes. She reaches home at 11:00 AM. What time does her tennis lesson begin?

10:00 AM

Kip played guitar at a talent show. He reached the town hall at 5:30 PM and rehearsed for 15 minutes. The show lasted 45 minutes. Then he spent 30 minutes at the refreshment stand and left. What time did Kip leave the town hall?

7:00 PM

Allie takes violin lessons for 30 minutes every Thursday. Her trip home takes 30 minutes. If she gets home at 6:00 PM, what time does her lesson begin?

5:00 PM

Use a toy clock or draw a clock on a small chalkboard and take turns displaying and identifying different times with your child. Encourage your child to say the time in different ways, "such as quarter past two" and "2:15."

Time Schedules ★

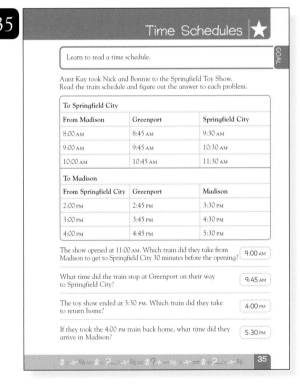

GOAL Learn to read a time schedule.

Aunt Kay took Nick and Bonnie to the Springfield Toy Show.
Read the train schedule and figure out the answer to each problem.

To Springfield City		
From Madison	Greenport	Springfield City
8:00 AM	8:45 AM	9:30 AM
9:00 AM	9:45 AM	10:30 AM
10:00 AM	10:45 AM	11:30 AM

To Madison		
From Springfield City	Greenport	Madison
2:00 PM	2:45 PM	3:30 PM
3:00 PM	3:45 PM	4:30 PM
4:00 PM	4:45 PM	5:30 PM

The show opened at 11:00 AM. Which train did they take from Madison to get to Springfield City 30 minutes before the opening?   9:00 AM

What time did the train stop at Greenport on their way to Springfield City?   9:45 AM

The toy show ended at 3:30 PM. Which train did they take to return home?   4:00 PM

If they took the 4:00 PM train back home, what time did they arrive in Madison?   5:30 PM

Find a train schedule at a local train station or online and use it to ask your child a few questions that will build his or her skills in reading and understanding real-life information.

★ Money Problems

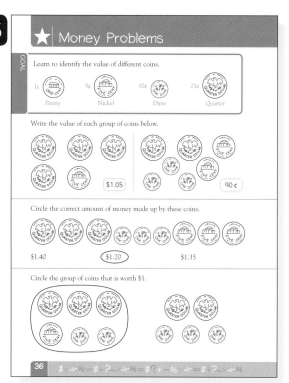

GOAL Learn to identify the value of different coins.

1¢ Penny 5¢ Nickel 10¢ Dime 25¢ Quarter

Write the value of each group of coins below.

$1.05

90¢

Circle the correct amount of money made up by these coins.

$1.40   **$1.20** $1.35

Circle the group of coins that is worth $1.

One of the most effective ways of teaching your child about money is to let him or her handle it. Let your child save money in a piggy bank or a see-through container. Try asking him or her to count the coins needed for a parking meter or vending machine, or let your child pay for his or her purchases at a yard sale or lemonade stand.

Money Problems ★

GOAL Learn to solve problems involving money.

Nina, Lisa, Harry, and Fernando went out for lunch with their dad. Look at the restaurant's menu and then figure out the answers.

Specials at Larry's Lunch Bunch	
Cheese sandwich	$2.50
Macaroni and cheese	$2.85
Chicken fingers	$3.25
Turkey taco	$3.50
Veggie burger	$3.00
Fries	$1.50
All drinks	$1.00

Dad ordered a cheese sandwich with fries and a drink. How much did his lunch cost? **$5**

Nina ordered chicken fingers, fries, and a drink. How much did her lunch cost? **$5.75**

Lisa ordered one of the specials along with fries. Her lunch cost $4. Which special did she order? **Cheese sandwich**

Harry had $5 to buy lunch. He ordered macaroni and cheese. How much money did he have left? **$2.15**

Fernando ordered a turkey taco, fries, and a drink. How much did his lunch cost? **$6**

How much did everyone's lunch cost in total? **$23.60**

You can discuss menus and prices during restaurant visits to teach your child about money. They offer a practical way of showing your child the importance of adding and subtracting money.

★ Shapes and Lines

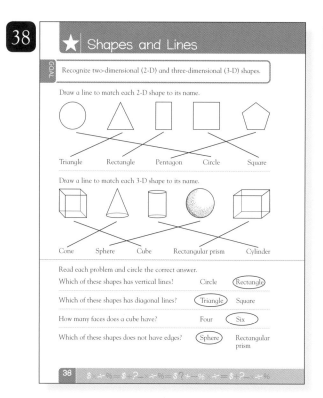

GOAL Recognize two-dimensional (2-D) and three-dimensional (3-D) shapes.

Draw a line to match each 2-D shape to its name.

Triangle   Rectangle   Pentagon   Circle   Square

Draw a line to match each 3-D shape to its name.

Cone   Sphere   Cube   Rectangular prism   Cylinder

Read each problem and circle the correct answer.

Which of these shapes has vertical lines?   Circle   **Rectangle**

Which of these shapes has diagonal lines?   **Triangle**   Square

How many faces does a cube have?   Four   **Six**

Which of these shapes does not have edges?   **Sphere**   Rectangular prism

To reinforce the concept of 2-D (flat) and 3-D shapes, show your child the differences between a drawing of a square or rectangle and a box, a drawing of a triangle and a triangular pyramid, and so on.

Fractions of Shapes ★

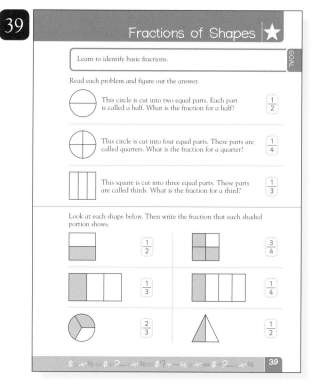

GOAL Learn to identify basic fractions.

Read each problem and figure out the answer.

This circle is cut into two equal parts. Each part is called a half. What is the fraction for a half? $\frac{1}{2}$

This circle is cut into four equal parts. These parts are called quarters. What is the fraction for a quarter? $\frac{1}{4}$

This square is cut into three equal parts. These parts are called thirds. What is the fraction for a third? $\frac{1}{3}$

Look at each shape below. Then write the fraction that each shaded portion shows.

$\frac{1}{2}$ $\frac{3}{4}$

$\frac{1}{3}$ $\frac{1}{4}$

$\frac{2}{3}$ $\frac{1}{2}$

Your child may not yet have learned about fractions. Go through this page slowly, answering any questions he or she may have. Using real-life objects to relate the concept of fractions may be helpful, such as a small pizza or pie cut into thirds or quarters.

★ Measure Objects

Learn to measure length in inches and centimeters.

Harry and Sally went fishing together. Use a ruler to measure what they found. Then write the answers to the nearest centimeter or inch in the boxes.

Harry had a worm for bait. He measured the worm.

It was [5] centimeters long.

A ladybug flew onto Harry's arm. Sally measured it.

It was [2] centimeters long.

After a long wait, Sally finally caught a fish. She measured it.

It was [4] inches long.

Harry caught a bigger fish than Sally. He measured it.

It was [5] inches long.

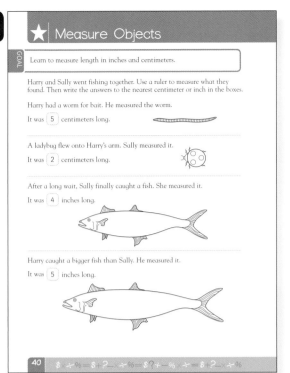

Learning to use measuring tools is not only a practical skill, but it is fun, too. As an extra activity, give your child several pieces of colorful yarn (precut to various lengths) to measure with a ruler.

Units of Length ★

Practice measuring length in inches and centimeters.

Mary bought two ribbons. How long is each one?
Measure them using a ruler and give your answer in inches.

[5] inches

[4] inches

How long are the two pieces of ribbon altogether? (5 + 4) = [9] inches

Josh picked up some leaves in the park. How long are they?
Measure them using a ruler and give your answer in centimeters.

[8] centimeters

[5] centimeters

How much longer is one leaf than the other? (8 – 5) = [3] centimeters

Anna has a piece of rope. How long is it? Use a ruler to measure it and give your answer in centimeters.

[16] centimeters

Can she make two equal length pieces from this piece of rope? Yes

How long would each piece be? [8] centimeters

Try playing a game: List ten items (a foot, a tree trunk, a doorway, a frying pan, and so on). Create two columns on a piece of paper, one for estimation and the other for measurement. Ask your child first to estimate the length of each item, and then to measure it. How close were the estimations?

★ Tally Marks

Learn to make tally marks on a graph to record the number of single items or groups of five items.

Kevin went hiking with his parents. He collected leaves along the trail and noted each type he found. He collected five oak leaves, eight hickory leaves, 19 dogwood leaves, 28 poplar leaves, and 35 ginkgo leaves. Make tally marks on the graph below to show the number of leaves collected. The first one has been done for you.

| = 1 leaf
卌 = 5 leaves

Leaves Collected by Kevin

Type of Leaf		Number of Leaves
Oak	🌱	卌
Hickory	🍃	卌 |||
Dogwood	🍂	卌 卌 卌 ||||
Poplar	🍁	卌 卌 卌 卌 卌 |||
Ginkgo	🍀	卌 卌 卌 卌 卌 卌 卌

Look carefully at the tally marks above to answer these questions.

How many oak leaves did Kevin collect? [5] leaves

How many more dogwood than hickory leaves did he collect? [11] leaves

Which leaves are 15 + 4 in number? Dogwood leaves

Which leaves are 30 + 5 in number? Ginkgo leaves

Which leaves are 23 more in number than oak leaves? Poplar leaves

The tally system is a quick, handy way of showing data in groups of fives. Tallying helps your child gain proficiency in adding—and, later, in multiplying—by fives.

Tally Marks ★

Reinforce understanding of tally marks on graphs.

The children in Ms. Garcia's class went on a field trip to the beach. Each child collected shells. Ellen collected six shells, Jack collected nine, Augie collected 12, and Joseph collected 15. Use tally marks to show how many shells each child collected. The first one has been done for you.

| = 1 shell
卌 = 5 shells

Shells Collected by Children

Child	Number of Shells
Ellen	卌 |
Jack	卌 ||||
Augie	卌 卌 ||
Joseph	卌 卌 卌

Look carefully at the tally marks above to answer these questions.

Who collected the most shells? Joseph

Which two children collected a total of 15 shells? Ellen and Jack

Which child collected twice as many shells as Ellen? Augie

Which child collected three more shells than Augie? Joseph

Which two children collected 27 shells altogether? Augie and Joseph

What was the total number of shells collected? [42] shells

Reinforce the concept of tallying by asking your child to count the letters in the name of his or her street, town, and school. Learning to identify and show data is a key skill in math and science.

★ Bar Graphs

Learn to understand the information shown on a bar graph.

Mr. Reed asked his students about the types of books they read last summer. He made a bar graph to show which types they liked best.

Students' Favorite Books

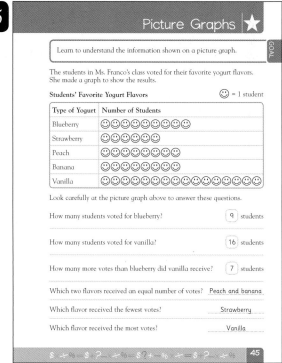

Look carefully at the bar graph above to answer these questions.

Which type of books received the fewest votes?
Sports

Which type of books received the same number of votes as science books?
Adventure

Which type of books received more votes than sports but fewer than mystery?
Biography

Which two types of books received a total of 15 votes?
Animal and biography

Graphs are a great way to record and display data. With your child, design a graph to collect data about a topic that interests him or her.

Picture Graphs ★

Learn to understand the information shown on a picture graph.

The students in Ms. Franco's class voted for their favorite yogurt flavors. She made a graph to show the results.

Students' Favorite Yogurt Flavors   ☺ = 1 student

Type of Yogurt	Number of Students
Blueberry	☺☺☺☺☺☺☺☺☺
Strawberry	☺☺☺☺☺
Peach	☺☺☺☺☺☺☺☺
Banana	☺☺☺☺☺☺☺☺
Vanilla	☺☺☺☺☺☺☺☺☺☺☺☺☺☺☺☺

Look carefully at the picture graph above to answer these questions.

How many students voted for blueberry? 9 students

How many students voted for vanilla? 16 students

How many more votes than blueberry did vanilla receive? 7 students

Which two flavors received an equal number of votes? Peach and banana

Which flavor received the fewest votes? Strawberry

Which flavor received the most votes? Vanilla

Point out that a picture graph uses pictures instead of numbers to display information. In this way, information can be seen and counted more easily. Explain that a graph has a title, which describes the information shown, and a key, which tells you what each picture represents.

★ More Picture Graphs

Learn to record information on a picture graph.

Ms. Green's students voted for their favorite vegetable. Ten students voted for corn, eight for cucumber, five for carrot, five for peas, and three for broccoli. Draw a picture graph to show the results. Create a key, give each column a heading, and give your graph a title.

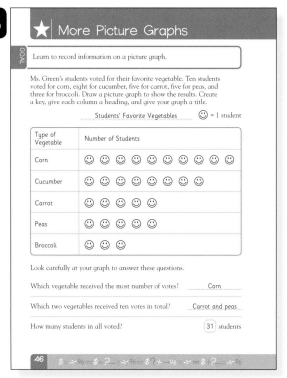

Look carefully at your graph to answer these questions.

Which vegetable received the most number of votes? Corn

Which two vegetables received ten votes in total? Carrot and peas

How many students in all voted? 31 students

Look through magazines, newspapers, or the Internet with your child for examples of picture graphs. Ask him or her if he or she can explain to you the information that they show.

More Picture Graphs ★

Reinforce your understanding of picture graphs.

Mr. Sanjay asked his students to raise their hands to vote for their favorite subjects. He made a graph to show the results.

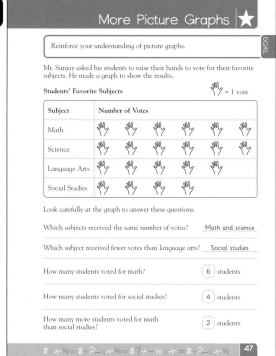

Look carefully at the graph to answer these questions.

Which subjects received the same number of votes? Math and science

Which subject received fewer votes than language arts? Social studies

How many students voted for math? 6 students

How many students voted for social studies? 4 students

How many more students voted for math than social studies? 2 students

You can ask your child to create graphs at home to keep track of the weather, friends' birthdays, a toy car collection, a doll collection, or other information. Graphing a subject your child can relate to will keep him or her engaged.